Tristan
and Isolde

STARTER LEVEL   250 HEADWORDS

OXFORD
UNIVERSITY PRESS

Great Clarendon Street, Oxford OX2 6DP

Oxford University Press is a department of the University of Oxford.
It furthers the University's objective of excellence in research, scholarship,
and education by publishing worldwide in

Oxford New York

Auckland Cape Town Dar es Salaam Hong Kong Karachi
Kuala Lumpur Madrid Melbourne Mexico City Nairobi
New Delhi Shanghai Taipei Toronto

With offices in

Argentina Austria Brazil Chile Czech Republic France Greece
Guatemala Hungary Italy Japan Poland Portugal Singapore
South Korea Switzerland Thailand Turkey Ukraine Vietnam

OXFORD and OXFORD ENGLISH are registered trade marks of
Oxford University Press in the UK and in certain other countries

This edition © Oxford University Press 2010

The moral rights of the author have been asserted

Database right Oxford University Press (maker)

First published in Dominoes 2008

2014 2013

10 9 8 7 6 5 4

ISBN: 978 0 19 424713 9 BOOK
ISBN: 978 0 19 424677 4 BOOK AND MULTIROM PACK
MULTIROM NOT AVAILABLE SEPARATELY

No unauthorized photocopying

Any websites referred to in this publication are in the public domain and
their addresses are provided by Oxford University Press for information only.
Oxford University Press disclaims any responsibility for the content

Printed in China

This book is printed on paper from certified and well-managed sources.

ACKNOWLEDGEMENTS

For my father, John Bowler (1929–), former flautist at the Royal Opera House, Covent
Garden, who gave me my love of opera and of ballet

Illustrations and cover by: Brian Lee

The publisher would like to thank the following for permission to reproduce photographs: Alamy
Images pp42 (Tintagel Castle/Robert Estall Photo Agency), 43 (scary face/Brian Elliott), 44
(Kronberg Royal Castle, Denmark/Bernie Epstein), 44 (Crac des Chavaliers, Syria/Rex Allen),
44 (Dover Castle, Kent/Skyscan photolibrary); Aquarius Library p41 (*Moulin Rouge!*, 2001/
Twentieth Century Fox); iStockphoto p47 (Antique Book/Anja Kaiser); Ronald Grant Archive
p iv (Tristan & Isolde GER / CZECH / US / BR 2006]/C20th Fox / Apollopromedia Gmbh /
Epsilon Motion Pictures / Franchise Pictures / Qi Quality International Gmbh / Scott Free
Productions / Stillking Films / World 2000 Entertainment).

DOMINOES

Series Editors: Bill Bowler and Sue Parminter

Tristan and Isolde

Retold by Bill Bowler

Illustrated by Brian Lee

Bill Bowler studied English Literature at Cambridge University and mime in Paris before becoming an English language teacher, trainer, and materials writer. He loves the theatre, opera and ballet, cinema, history, art – and travelling. He also enjoys reading books and writing poetry in his free time. Bill lives in Alicante with his wife, Sue Parminter, and their three children. This Dominoes retelling of *Tristan and Isolde* is based partly on Wagner's opera (1865) and partly on older versions of the tale.

OXFORD
UNIVERSITY PRESS

BEFORE READING

1 **Here are some of the people in the story of *Tristan and Isolde*. Look at the pictures and complete the sentences.**

Tristan lives in Cornwall.

King Mark is Tristan's uncle.

Melot is Tristan's friend.

Isolde lives in Ireland.

Morold is Isolde's uncle.

Brangwain is Isolde's servant.

a Tristan lives with King Mark/Melot.

b Tristan is angry, and he kills Brangwain/Morold.

c Isolde/Melot helps Tristan when he is ill.

d Isolde/Brangwain loves King Mark/Tristan.

e Isolde marries King Mark/Tristan.

f Melot/Brangwain helps Isolde when she meets Tristan.

g King Mark/Melot hates Tristan, and wants to kill him.

2 ***Tristan and Isolde* is a love story. What happens in the end?**

a ☐ Tristan and Isolde marry and live happily.

b ☐ Tristan and Isolde die sadly from love.

c ☐ Tristan leaves Isolde when he meets a beautiful French woman.

Chapter 1   Tristan meets Isolde

When our story begins, **King** Anguish is the King of Ireland . . .

. . . and King Mark is the King of Cornwall.

Ireland is a bigger country than Cornwall . . .

. . . and so every year King Mark must give money to King Anguish's brother, Morold, and his men.

king the most important man in a country

One year, King Mark is late with the money. Morold is angry when he comes to Cornwall for it. 'The money for my brother is late,' he says. 'So this year you must pay more.'

Tristan, King Mark's **nephew**, is angry with Morold. 'You must **fight** me,' he says, 'before you can take the money.'

Morold fights Tristan. Morold's **sword** has **poison** on it . . .

. . . but Tristan kills him.

---

nephew your sister's (or brother's) son

fight to hit someone again and again

sword a long, sharp knife for fighting

poison something that kills people when they eat or drink it

Morold's men take his dead body home. Now Cornwall and Ireland are **at war**.

Tristan's **wound** does not get better. His **servant** Kurvenal puts him in a **boat** and they go to look for help.

They go across the sea to Ireland. There, Tristan meets Isolde, the daughter of King Anguish. 'What's your name?' she asks. He doesn't give his true name to her. 'Tramtris,' he says.

at war when two countries are fighting

wound a hole in the body from a knife or a sword

servant a person who works for someone rich

boat you go across water in this

When Isolde sees Tristan's wound she wants to help him.
'Drink this,' she says, and she gives him a **potion**.

With her potions, Isolde makes Tristan better. At the same time, they **fall in love**.

But one day Isolde is looking at Tristan's sword. A little **piece** of it is **missing**.

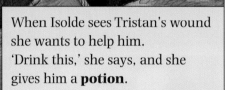

She goes and finds a little piece of a sword. It comes from her **uncle** Morold's dead body. It is the missing piece from Tristan's sword. 'So he isn't Tramtris. He's Tristan – my uncle's killer!' she says.

---

potion something that you drink to make you better, love someone, or die

fall in love to begin loving

piece some, but not all, of something

missing not there

uncle your father's (or mother's) brother

t first Isolde is angry. She wants to
ll Tristan. But she's in love with him.
she says nothing to her father.

Tristan goes back to Ireland, but he isn't happy. Peace with Ireland is important, but Tristan loves Isolde, and he wants to marry her. He doesn't want to get Isolde for his uncle.

After some time Tristan goes back to Cornwall. There he tells King Mark all about Isolde. 'She's beautiful,' he says.

King Mark wants **peace** with Ireland.
'Tristan,' he says, 'I must **marry** Isolde. Go back to Ireland and bring her to me.'

peace not fighting

marry to make someone your wife or husband

READING CHECK

Complete the sentences with the correct names.

a Tristan lives in Cornwall with his uncle, King Mark .

b When .... asks for more money, ... kills him.

c .... and .... go across the sea to Ireland.

d .... makes Tristan better.

e .... and .... fall in love.

f .... is angry when he/she finds Tristan's sword.

g Isolde doesn't tell .... about Morold's killer.

h .... isn't happy when he/she goes back to Ireland.

WORD WORK

1 Find words from Chapter 1 to complete the sentences.

a Morold is Isolde's u n c l e .

b Tristan is King Mark's n _ _ _ _ _ .

c Morold doesn't kill Tristan, but there's p _ _ _ _ _ on his sword.

d Tristan's w _ _ _ _ gets better when he drinks Isolde's p _ _ _ _ _ .

e When two people f _ _ _ i _ l _ _ _ , they usually want to marry.

f 'Where's your bicycle?' 'I don't know! It's m _ _ _ _ _ _ .'

g 'Are you hungry? Would you like a p _ _ _ _ of bread?'

h Many people want p _ _ _ _ when their country is a _ w _ _ .

2 These pictures don't match the words. Correct them.

a ~~king~~ _sword_

b marry ....

c servant ....

d sword ....

e boat ....

f fight ....

GUESS WHAT

What happens in the next chapter? Tick two boxes.

a ☐ King Anguish fights Tristan.

b ☐ Isolde leaves Ireland to go to Cornwall.

c ☐ Isolde is happy to marry King Mark.

d ☐ Isolde wants to kill Tristan.

Chapter 2   Love and Hate

In Ireland, King Anguish listens to the **message** of peace from King Mark. 'And so my uncle wants to marry Isolde,' says Tristan in the end.

King Anguish thinks carefully about King Mark's message. Then he says, 'You're right. Take Isolde to King Mark. When they marry, our two countries can be at peace.'

Isolde doesn't want to marry King Mark, but she is a good daughter, and so she says goodbye to her father.

message something that one person tells another person to say to someone

That afternoon, Isolde goes **sadly** onto Tristan's **ship** with her **maid** Brangwain.

Isolde loves Tristan and she wants to marry him. In his **heart** Tristan loves Isolde, too, but she must marry his uncle. He knows that, and so he is cold and **unfriendly** to her.

When the ship is out at sea, Isolde tells Brangwain, 'Bring my potions to me.'

The potions come from Isolde's mother. Brangwain brings them at once.

sadly not happily

maid a woman who works in a rich person's house

ship a big boat

heart the centre of feeling in someone

unfriendly not nice

9

Isolde takes two bottles from the box. 'This bottle with the heart is a love potion,' she tells Brangwain. 'I must drink it when I marry King Mark. And this black bottle is poison.'

'Poison?' says Brangwain. She is afraid.

'Tristan doesn't love me now,' Isolde says angrily. 'He's taking me to Cornwall, and there I must marry his uncle.'

She gives the black bottle to Brangwain. 'Put this in a **cup** for Tristan. I want to kill him!' she says.

Brangwain is afraid. Perhaps Isolde wants to die with Tristan, she thinks. What can she do?

cup you drink from this

Tristan comes and speaks to Isolde.
'Thank you for **looking after** me in Ireland,' he says.
'I don't understand,' she answers. 'Why are you cold and unfriendly with me now?'
'I'm sorry,' says Tristan. 'But you must marry my uncle. So our old love is **impossible**.'

'I **hate** you,' says Isolde angrily.
'Then kill me,' says Tristan, and he gives his sword to her.
'No, not with your sword,' says Isolde.

Just then, Brangwain brings a cup to Isolde. Isolde gives the cup to Tristan. 'Drink this!' she says.
Tristan takes the cup and begins to drink. He is ready to die. But before he can finish the potion, Isolde quickly takes the cup from his hand. She drinks from it, too.

look after to do things for someone or something that needs help   **impossible** what cannot be   **hate** not to love

READING CHECK

Put the sentences into the correct order. Number them 1–9.

a ☐ Tristan comes and speaks to Isolde.

b ☐ Brangwain brings potions to Isolde.

c ☐ Tristan gives King Mark's message of peace to King Anguish.

d ☐ Isolde gives a cup to Tristan, and says, 'Drink this!'

e ☐ Isolde says goodbye to her father.

f ☐ Tristan gives his sword to Isolde.

g ☐ Isolde and Brangwain go onto Tristan's ship.

h ☐ Isolde takes the cup from Tristan and drinks from it, too.

i ☐ Isolde tells Brangwain, 'Put poison in a cup for Tristan.'

WORD WORK

1 Find eight more words from Chapter 2 in the cup.

2 Use the words from Activity 1 to complete these sentences.

a Don't drink from that ...... cup ...... ! There's poison in it.

b Please come to the office; there's a .... from your mother.

c 'Do you like cats?' 'No, I don't. I .... them.'

d Their .... cleans their house for them.

e 'My mother's dead,' he says ....

f Our love is .... We can never marry.

g I don't want to live in that town because the people there are very ....

h We're going across the Atlantic to America on a big ....

i Soon there is love for Juliet in Romeo's ....

GUESS WHAT

What happens in the next chapter? Tick one box.

Tristan and Isolde . . .

a ☐ . . . die.

b ☐ . . . fall in love again.

c ☐ . . . marry.

d ☐ . . . go back to Ireland.

Chapter 3   Isolde's Wedding

Suddenly Tristan and Isolde's hearts are **full** of love again.

'I love you,' says Isolde.
'And I love you, too,' says Tristan.

They **kiss**.

'What's happening?' asks Isolde.
'It's the work of the love potion and not the poison, my **lady**,' says Brangwain. 'I'm sorry.'

'Don't be sorry, Brangwain,' smiles Isolde. 'I feel happy because my heart is full of true love for Tristan again.'

full with lots of something in

kiss to touch lovingly with your mouth

lady an important woman from a good family

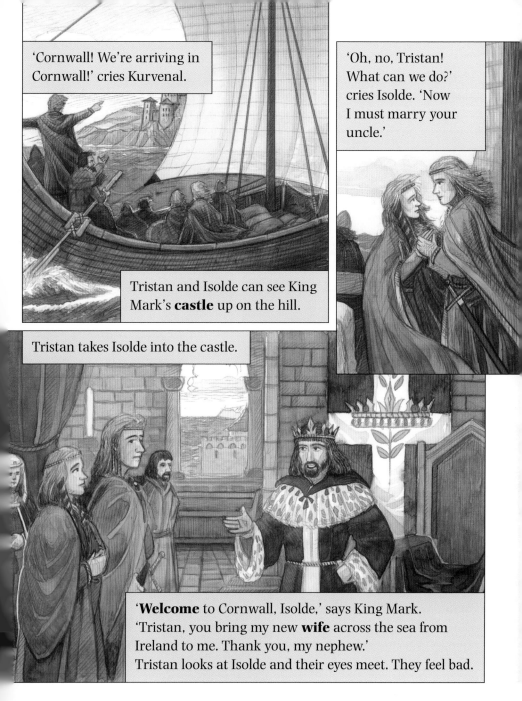

'Cornwall! We're arriving in Cornwall!' cries Kurvenal.

'Oh, no, Tristan! What can we do?' cries Isolde. 'Now I must marry your uncle.'

Tristan and Isolde can see King Mark's **castle** up on the hill.

Tristan takes Isolde into the castle.

'**Welcome** to Cornwall, Isolde,' says King Mark. 'Tristan, you bring my new **wife** across the sea from Ireland to me. Thank you, my nephew.'
Tristan looks at Isolde and their eyes meet. They feel bad.

castle a big old building; a rich person lives here

welcome we say this when someone arrives and we are happy to see them

wife a woman living with a man

15

The next day is King Mark's **wedding** day. Isolde marries the king, but in her heart she doesn't love him. She loves Tristan.

At the wedding **feast**, Isolde calls Brangwain to her. 'Brangwain, you must help me after the feast,' she says.

'Of course, my lady,' says Brangwain.

Later, King Mark and his new wife, Isolde, leave the wedding feast. 'Goodnight Tristan, goodnight my good friends,' says the king.

King Mark is drinking with Tristan and Tristan's friend, Melot. The king is very happy.

'Goodnight Tristan,' says Isolde quietly.

wedding the time when two people marry

feast a lot of good things to eat

King Mark and Isolde go to the king's room. Brangwain goes with them.

In the king's room, Isolde gets ready for bed.

'Brangwain,' says Isolde. '**Put out** the **torches** for us.'
'Yes, my lady,' says Brangwain.

In the dark, Brangwain goes to the king's bed . . .

. . . and Isolde leaves the king's room.

put out to stop something burning

torch it burns and gives light: in the past people used them to see at night

READING CHECK

Are these sentences true or false? Tick the boxes.

		True	False
a	When Tristan and Isolde drink the love potion in the cup, they fall in love again.	☑	☐
b	Isolde is angry about the love potion.	☐	☐
c	Tristan takes Isolde to King Mark's castle.	☐	☐
d	Isolde loves King Mark when she marries him.	☐	☐
e	Kurvenal goes to the king's room with King Mark and Isolde.	☐	☐
f	When Brangwain goes to the king's bed, it is dark.	☐	☐
g	Isolde leaves the king's room.	☐	☐

WORD WORK

1 Find words from Chapter 3 to match the pictures.

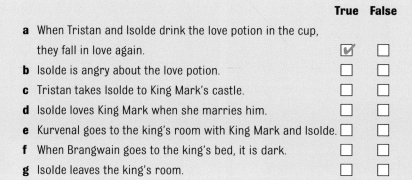

a c a s t l e

b p _ _ o _ _

c k _ _ _

d t _ _ _ _ _ _

e w _ _ _ _ _ _

f w _ _ _

g l _ _ _

h f _ _ _ _

i f _ _ _

2 Use words from Activity 1 to complete Brangwain's diary.

Today is Isolde's (a) ..wedding.. day, and now she is King Mark's
(b) .... But my (c) .... isn't happy. Her heart is
(d) .... of love for Tristan! At the wedding (e) ....,
Isolde asks for my help. We go to the king's room, and I
(f) .... the (g) .... there. Then Isolde leaves the
dark room, and goes through the (h) .... to Tristan. When
they meet, they (i) ...., I know.

GUESS WHAT

What happens in the next chapter? Match the two parts of the sentences.

a Tristan often meets . . .

b Tristan visits Isolde when . . .

c Melot sees . . .

d Melot speaks to . . .

e Tristan and Isolde are lovers but . . .

1 Tristan and Isolde when they kiss.

2 King Mark doesn't know it.

3 King Mark about Tristan.

4 Brangwain puts out the torch.

5 Isolde in the castle.

Chapter 4   Melot is not a True Friend

Tristan is a good singer, and he plays the **harp** well. All the ladies in King Mark's castle like him a lot.

King Mark likes Tristan a lot too. They often **hunt together**.

At the castle, Melot is Tristan's best friend.

But, Melot is not a true friend. He is **jealous** of Tristan.
'Everyone loves Tristan,' he thinks.
'But I don't. I hate him.'

harp you make music on this instrument by pulling the strings with your fingers

hunt to look for and kill animals

together with someone or near to someone

jealous feeling angry or sad because you want to have what someone has

When King Mark meets his **lords** in the castle . . .

. . . Tristan often meets Isolde in the garden. They walk and talk and laugh together. Melot watches them.

When King Mark is hunting . . .

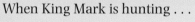

. . . Tristan often meets Isolde in the castle. He plays the harp and sings to her. Melot watches them there, too.

lord an important man from a good family

After some time, Melot goes to the king. 'Be careful, King Mark. Tristan and Isolde are in love!' he says.

The king doesn't **believe** Melot's stories. 'Tristan is my good nephew. He looks after Isolde when I'm **busy**. They aren't lovers. You're wrong,' he says.

One evening, Melot is in the garden near Isolde's room. Isolde is talking with Brangwain, and Melot listens.

'Of course,' says Isolde. 'Brangwain, put out the torch by my window and give him the **signal**.'
'Yes, my lady,' says Brangwain. She goes and takes the torch from Isolde's window.

'King Mark is busy tonight, Brangwain,' says Isolde. 'He's hunting with his lords.'
'Is Tristan coming to your room, my lady?' asks Brangwain.

believe to think that something is true

busy with a lot of things to do

signal something that you do to show someone a message from far away

22

At the same time Tristan is looking out of the window in his room. He sees Brangwain at Isolde's window. She puts out the torch. 'Good!' thinks Tristan. 'I can visit Isolde now.'

Tristan goes quickly to Isolde. They kiss when they meet.

Melot sees Tristan and Isolde together. He watches their kiss. 'I must tell the king about this,' he thinks.

READING CHECK

What do they say?

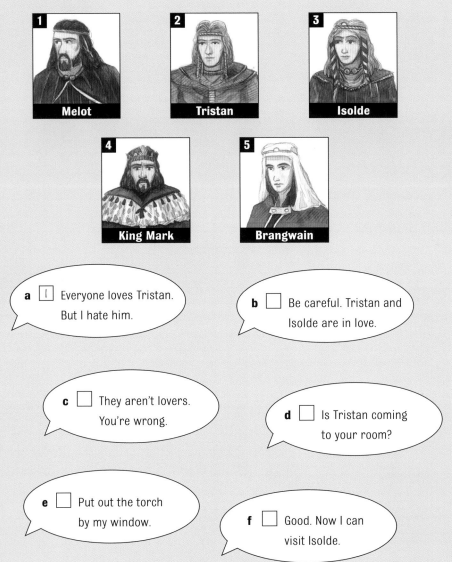

a ☐ Everyone loves Tristan. But I hate him.

b ☐ Be careful. Tristan and Isolde are in love.

c ☐ They aren't lovers. You're wrong.

d ☐ Is Tristan coming to your room?

e ☐ Put out the torch by my window.

f ☐ Good. Now I can visit Isolde.

WORD WORK

Find the words in the torch to complete the sentences.

a King Mark leaves the castle to h*unt*............. .

b Melot is not a true friend because he is j.................
of Tristan.

c When Tristan meets Isolde, he sings and plays the
h.................. .

d King Mark goes hunting with his l.................. .

e Brangwain puts out the torch and gives the s.................
to Tristan.

f Tristan is a good nephew, King Mark b.................. .

g Tristan and Isolde are in love; so they always want to be
t.................. .

h King Mark is happy when Tristan l.................
a................. Isolde.

i When King Mark is b................., Tristan and Isolde
can meet.

htun

eojalsu

prah

dorsl

ligans

levibese

gotehret

okslo faret

syub

GUESS WHAT

What happens in the next chapter? Put the sentences in order. Number them 1–5.

a ☐ King Mark comes back to the castle early.

b ☐ Tristan sees the signal and visits Isolde.

c ☐ King Mark leaves the castle to go hunting.

d ☐ Isolde puts out the torch.

e ☐ King Mark sees Tristan and Isolde together.

The next day, Melot speaks to King Mark about Tristan and Isolde's kiss.

Again the king does not believe Melot's story. 'It isn't true,' he says. 'Tristan is my nephew and he loves me. You're **lying**!'

Some days after that, King Mark and Isolde are eating in the early evening.

'You don't believe me, my lord, I can see,' he says. 'So, shall we **test** your nephew?' 'Test Tristan?' says King Mark. 'Yes, my lord,' says Melot, and he tells his **plan** to the king.

lie to say something that is not true   **test** to do something to someone to learn what they can do   **plan** when you get something ready before it happens

'Isolde, I'm hunting with my lords tonight,' says the King. 'We want to hunt all night and we're coming back to the castle early tomorrow morning. Good night.'

'Good night, my lord,' says Isolde, and she kisses the king.

The king **rides** out of the castle with twelve of his lords. Melot is riding next to him.

Later that evening, Isolde speaks to her maid. 'Brangwain, the king is busy tonight. Put out the torch. I want to see Tristan.'
'Don't call Tristan tonight, my lady,' says Brangwain. 'I don't **trust** Melot.'
'What are you saying?' cries Isolde. 'Melot is Tristan's good friend. Put out the torch, I say.'

ride to go on a horse

trust to believe that someone is nice and good

'No, my lady,' says Brangwain, and she runs from the room. So Isolde puts out the torch and waits for Tristan.

When Tristan arrives, he and Isolde kiss. Suddenly Tristan's servant Kurvenal arrives. 'The King! King Mark is coming!' he cries.

Just then Melot, the king, and his lords arrive. They aren't hunting all night. They are back at the castle early.
'You see, my lord, I am right about Tristan,' says Melot with a dark smile.

King Mark speaks sadly to Isolde, 'How can you do this to me? You are my wife. I am your **husband**.' Isolde says nothing to him.

Then King Mark says to his nephew, 'Tristan, how can you do this to me? I am your uncle, and your king.'

'I don't know,' says Tristan sadly. 'But I am ready to die for it.'

'And I am ready to die with you,' says Isolde. And she kisses Tristan in front of King Mark.

husband the man that a woman marries

READING CHECK

Correct the mistakes in the sentences.

King Mark

a Melot speaks to ~~Kurvenal~~ about Tristan and Isolde's kiss.

b King Mark believes Melot's story about Tristan.

c The king goes hunting with his lords in the morning.

d Brangwain wants to put out the torch.

e When King Mark comes back, Melot and Isolde are together.

f Isolde fights Tristan in front of King Mark.

WORD WORK

Complete the dialogues with words from Chapter 5.

a A: I'd like to go hunting with you.
B: Well, can you r.ide............. a horse?

b C: Can you t...................
your new maid?
D: Yes. She always looks after
my children when I go away.

c E: Do your teachers
t.................. you every week?
F: Yes. And when we don't do well,
they're angry with us!

d G: He's eighteen years old, he says.

H: He's I.................. . He's only

fifteen. I know – because he's my

nephew!

e I: Have you got any

p.................. for the weekend?

J: Yes. I'm going to buy a dress for my

sister's wedding.

f K: Do you know Paul?

L: Yes, of course. He's Carmen's

h.................. .

GUESS WHAT

What happens in the next chapter? Tick the boxes.

a Melot . . .

  1 ☐ kills Tristan.

  2 ☐ fights Tristan, but doesn't kill him.

  3 ☐ leaves King Mark's castle.

b Tristan . . .

  1 ☐ leaves Cornwall and forgets Isolde.

  2 ☐ leaves Cornwall, but cannot forget Isolde.

  3 ☐ marries Brangwain.

c Isolde . . .

  1 ☐ marries Tristan.

  2 ☐ never sees Tristan again.

  3 ☐ dies with Tristan.

Chapter 6 Lovers Forever

Angrily Melot **stabs** Tristan in the back with his **dagger**. There's poison on it.

Tristan **falls**, but Kurvenal helps him. 'Take my nephew away from here **forever**,' cries King Mark angrily. 'I never want to see him again.'
Isolde cries and cries, but she can do nothing for her lover.

Kurvenal takes Tristan away in his ship. After some time, they arrive in Brittany.

stab to push a knife into someone   **fall** to go down suddenly   **forever** for all time
dagger a knife for killing people

There, the daughter of King Howell of Brittany looks after Tristan. Her name is Blanche.

Soon Blanche falls in love with Tristan. But Tristan cannot forget his love for Isolde. He thinks about her all the time.

After many months, the wound from Melot's dagger does not get better. Tristan calls Kurvenal and gives a **letter** to him. 'I can't live without Isolde. Take this letter to her,' he says. 'I'm asking her to come here to me.'

'And, Kurvenal, can you do something when you come back?' asks Tristan.

'Of course, my lord,' says Kurvenal. 'What is it?'

letter you write this to tell something to someone

'With Isolde on your ship, put up a white **sail**,' says Tristan. 'Then I can know the good **news** at once when I see the ship far away. Without Isolde on your ship, put up a black sail.'

'Yes, my lord,' says Kurvenal.

At the door of the room, Blanche listens carefully to Tristan's **words**.

When Kurvenal arrives at King Mark's castle in Cornwall, he speaks with Isolde and gives Tristan's letter to her.

Isolde reads the letter. 'Isolde, my love, only you can help me!' it says. 'Please come and **save** me, with love from your Tristan.'

sail this uses wind to help something to move

news when someone tells you something new

word a thing that you say or write

save to stop bad things happening to someone or something

34

Isolde goes at once and speaks with her husband, King Mark.

'Your nephew, Tristan, is dying,' she tells him. 'The wound in his back is full of poison from Melot's dagger. Only I can save him. Can I go to him?'

The king loves his wife, Isolde, very much, but in his heart he also loves his nephew, Tristan.

'Yes, Isolde, you can,' King Mark says sadly. 'Go to him and help him. You must save him!'

Some days later, Kurvenal's ship arrives in Brittany. A **shepherd** on the hill near King Howell's castle sees it and cries, 'A ship, a ship!'

In his room in the castle, Tristan hears the shepherd's cry. He is very ill and he can't get up from his bed.

'Go to the window!' he tells Blanche. 'What can you see?'

shepherd a man who looks after sheep

Blanche goes to the window and looks out. 'I can see a ship!' she says. 'And it's coming nearer and nearer!' 'Are the sails white or black?' Tristan asks her.

Blanche remembers Tristan's words to Kurvenal. She sees the white sails on Kurvenal's ship, but she is jealous of Tristan's love for Isolde.

'The sails are black,' she lies.

'Oh no! I can't believe it. She isn't coming!' cries Tristan. Suddenly he sits up in bed, puts his hand to his heart, and dies.

Blanche runs from the room, afraid.

Just then, Isolde arrives with Kurvenal and Brangwain. She sits on Tristan's bed, and takes him in her arms. But he is dead and she cannot save him now.

With a cry, Isolde's heart **breaks**, and her dead body falls next to Tristan's.

Kurvenal and Brangwain **bury** Isolde next to Tristan. From Tristan's **grave** a white **rose grows** and from Isolde's grave a red rose grows. The roses grow together. Tristan and Isolde are dead, but their love lives forever.

break to make one thing into many little parts

bury to put a dead body under the ground

grave where you bury someone

rose a flower, red or white in colour; people often give roses to lovers

grow to begin living and to get bigger

READING CHECK

Match the first and second parts of the sentences.

a Melot wants to kill Tristan but . . .

b King Mark is angry and . . .

c Blanche looks after Tristan and . . .

d Tristan writes a letter because . . .

e When Isolde reads Tristan's letter . . .

f Kurvenal takes Isolde to Brittany and . . .

g Blanche lies to Tristan because . . .

h Isolde takes Tristan in her arms, but . . .

i Tristan and Isolde die, but . . .

1 she wants to go to him.

2 their love lives forever.

3 he puts white sails on his ship.

4 she falls in love with him.

5 Tristan doesn't die.

6 she cannot save him.

7 he cannot live without Isolde.

8 he never wants to see Tristan again.

9 she is jealous.

WORD WORK

1 Find fourteen more words from Chapter 6 in the grave stones.

2 Match the definitions with words from Activity 1.

a to put a dead body in the ground ......bury......

b a short sword ....

c this man looks after sheep ....

d to stop bad things happening to someone ....

e to go down suddenly ....

f this moves a ship ....

g when you hear something new ....

h for all time ....

i you say or write this ....

j you bury someone here ....

k people often give this flower to someone they love ....

l you write this to tell something to someone ....

m to live and get bigger ....

n to change into many parts ....

o to push a dagger into someone ....

3 Use the extra letters in the grave stones on page 38 to complete this sentence.

'T _ _ _ _ _ _ / A _ _ / I _ _ _ _ _'/ I _ / A/ V _ _ _/

G _ _ _ / O _ _ _ _ / B _ / R _ _ _ _ _ _ / W _ _ _ _ _.

GUESS WHAT

This story ends sadly. Which different ending do you like best?

a ☐ Blanche doesn't lie, and Isolde
     helps Tristan to get better.

b ☐ Tristan dies, and Isolde goes
     back to King Mark.

c ☐ Tristan dies, and Isolde goes
     back to Cornwall and kills Melot.

d ☐ Isolde doesn't come to Brittany,
     and Tristan learns to love Blanche.

Project A   *Sad love stories*

1 **Complete the story of *Tristan and Isolde* with the phrases in the box.**

after   at once   in the end   later   soon   when

a   Isolde looks after Tristan's wound and very .... they fall in love.

b   .... their love is impossible because Tristan's uncle, King Mark, marries Isolde.

c   .... the wedding, Tristan often meets Isolde in the castle.

d   .... King Mark finds out that Tristan and Isolde are lovers, he is very angry.

e   Tristan leaves King Mark's castle ...., but he cannot live without Isolde.

f   .... Tristan and Isolde die because their hearts break.

2 **Look at the story of *Romeo and Juliet*. Complete the story with the sentence halves that follow.**

1 When Romeo and Juliet meet at a party, . . . ☐

2 Soon their love is impossible because . . . ☐

3 After their secret wedding . . . ☐

4 Later Romeo gets the wrong message and . . . ☐

5 At once he goes to Juliet's grave and . . . ☐

6 In the end, Juliet . . . ☐

a . . . their two families are at war.

b . . . puts Romeo's dagger through her heart and dies.

c . . . they fall in love at once.

d . . . Romeo must leave the city.

e . . . he thinks, 'Juliet is dead!'

f . . . drinks poison there, and dies near her body.

3 Write a sad love story. Use these phrases to help you.

When they meet . . .

At once . . .

Soon . . .

Later their love is impossible because . . .

After . . .

In the end . . .

Project B — *Famous castles*

1 Look at the Tintagel Castle web page and complete the table below.

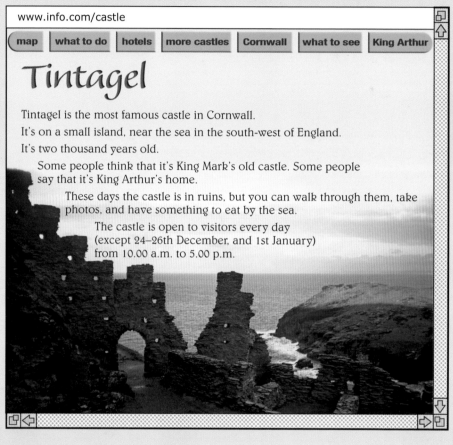

www.info.com/castle

| map | what to do | hotels | more castles | Cornwall | what to see | King Arthur |

Tintagel

Tintagel is the most famous castle in Cornwall.

It's on a small island, near the sea in the south-west of England.

It's two thousand years old.

Some people think that it's King Mark's old castle. Some people say that it's King Arthur's home.

These days the castle is in ruins, but you can walk through them, take photos, and have something to eat by the sea.

The castle is open to visitors every day (except 24–26th December, and 1st January) from 10.00 a.m. to 5.00 p.m.

What's the name of the castle?	
Where is it?	
How old is it?	
Are there any stories about famous past owners?	
What can you do there now?	
When is it open to visitors?	

2 Look at the information about Bran castle and complete the web page.

What's the name of the castle?	*Bran Castle*
Where is it?	*on a hill above the village of Bran, in Transylvania, Romania*
How old is it?	*six hundred years old*
Are there any stories about famous past owners?	*Vlad Tepes (the real 'Count Dracula')*
What can you do there now?	*visit the museum, see the well, go up the towers*
When is it open to visitors?	*Tuesday–Sunday, from 9 a.m. to 4 p.m.*

www.info.com/castle

| map | what to do | hotels | more castles | Romania | what to see | Count Dracula |

Bran Castle

Bran is the most famous castle ....
....
....

It's on a ....

It's .... years old.

Some people think that it's ....
.... old castle.

These days ....
....

The castle is open to visitors ....
....
....

3 **Complete the table with information about a famous castle near you, or choose one of these castles.**

Elsinore Castle, Denmark

Dover Castle, England

Kerak Castle, Jordan

What's the name of the castle?	
Where is it?	
How old is it?	
Are there any stories about famous past owners?	
What can you do there now?	
When is it open to visitors?	

4 **Make a web page about your famous castle. Use your notes to help you.**

www.info.com/castle

| map | what to do | hotels | more castles | what to see |

GRAMMAR CHECK

Present Simple: Yes/No questions and short answers

We use auxiliary verbs and be (main verb) in Yes/No questions.

Do you like Tristan and Isolde?

Is Tristan from Ireland?

In the short answer we reuse the auxiliary verb and be (main verb).

Yes, I do.

No, he isn't. (is not)

1 Write answers for the questions about Isolde. Use the short answers in the box.

No, she can't.	No, she doesn't.	No, she hasn't.	No, she isn't.	Yes, she can.
Yes, she does.	Yes, she does.	~~Yes, she is.~~	Yes, she is.	Yes, she has.

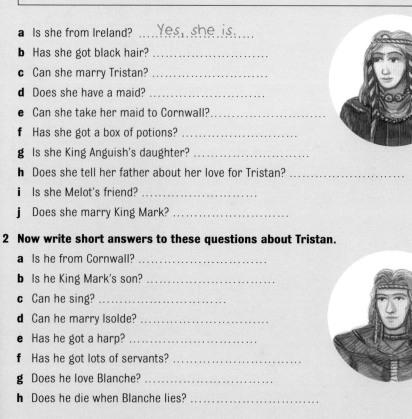

a Is she from Ireland? .....Yes, she is.....

b Has she got black hair? ....

c Can she marry Tristan? ....

d Does she have a maid? ....

e Can she take her maid to Cornwall?...........................

f Has she got a box of potions? ....

g Is she King Anguish's daughter? ....

h Does she tell her father about her love for Tristan? ....

i Is she Melot's friend? ....

j Does she marry King Mark? ....

2 Now write short answers to these questions about Tristan.

a Is he from Cornwall? ....

b Is he King Mark's son? ....

c Can he sing? ....

d Can he marry Isolde? ....

e Has he got a harp? ....

f Has he got lots of servants? ....

g Does he love Blanche? ....

h Does he die when Blanche lies? ....

GRAMMAR CHECK

Information questions and question words

We use question words in information questions.

What's the name of Isolde's mother?

How many brothers does King Anguish have?

Why does Melot hate Tristan?

We answer these questions by giving some information.

I don't know.

One, I think — Morold.

Because he's bad and Tristan's good.

3 Complete the information questions with the question words in the box.

How	How many	How much	What
When	Where	Which	Who	Who	Why

a Q: ......Who...... is Tristan's uncle?

A: King Mark.

b Q: .... does Tristan meet Isolde?

A: In Ireland.

c Q: .... does Tristan go back to Ireland?

A: Because King Mark asks him.

d Q: .... is Kurvenal?

A: Tristan's servant.

e Q: .... bottle has poison in it?

A: The black bottle.

f Q: .... love potion does Tristan drink?

A: Half a cup.

g Q: .... does Melot hit Tristan?

A: He stabs him in the back.

h Q: .... fights does Tristan have in the story?

A: Two. One with Morold and one with Melot.

i Q: .... does Tristan go to Brittany?

A: After King Mark learns about him and Isolde.

j Q: .... can we see on Tristan and Isolde's graves?

A: Red and white roses.

GRAMMAR CHECK

Verb + infinitive or –ing form

After the verbs *begin, forget, learn, like, need, remember, want* and *would like* we use the infinitive with *to*.

I'd like to read that book.

After the verbs *begin, finish, go, like, love,* and *stop* we use verb + –ing.

I love reading.

4 **Complete these sentences about the story with the *to* + infinitive or verb + –*ing* form of the verb in brackets.**

  a From her mother Isolde learns .to make. (make) people better with potions.

  b Isolde begins .... (love) Tristan when he is very ill.

  c Tristan stops .... (say) nice things to Isolde when he goes back to Ireland for his uncle.

  d Brangwain likes .... (help) Isolde.

  e King Mark often goes .... (hunt) in the evening.

  f Tristan loves .... (sing).

  g Tristan and Isolde need .... (meet) when King Mark is far away.

  h Brangwain doesn't want .... (put) out the torch by Isolde's window.

  i Isolde forgets .... (be) careful when she meets Tristan.

  j King Mark would like .... (save) Tristan in the end.

  k Kurvenal remembers .... (have) white sails up on his boat before he takes Isolde to Brittany.

  l Blanche finishes .... (look) after Tristan when he dies.

  m Kurvenal likes .... (work) for Tristan.

  n Tristan learns .... (play) the harp when he is young.

  o Melot begins .... (talk) to King Mark about Tristan and Isolde behind Tristan's back.

GRAMMAR CHECK

Prepositions of movement

Prepositions of movement tell us how something moves.

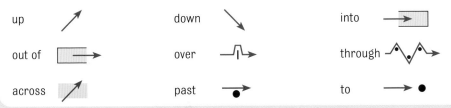

up	down	into
out of	over	through
across	past	to

5 How can Tristan go to Isolde? Complete the text with the prepositions in the box.

| across | down | into | ~~out of~~ | out of |
| over | past | through | to | up |

Tristan must go a) ..... out of ..... his room and b)............... the castle garden.
He must go c)............... the castle and d)............... the road. Then he must go right,
e)............... the hill and f)............... the trees. After that he must go g)...............
the shepherd's house and down h)............... the water. In the end he must go
i)............... the water and j)............... the old boatman's house.

GRAMMAR CHECK

Present Simple: affirmative

With most verbs in the Present Simple, we add –s to make the *he/she/it* form of the verb.

Later Isolde arrives at King Mark's castle.

Tristan plays the harp.

After the verbs *go*, *finish*, *kiss*, *teach* and *watch* we add –es.

Isolde's mother teaches her about potions.

When verbs end in consonant + –y such as *bury*, *cry*, *marry*, we change y into i and add –es.

Isolde cries when Tristan leaves Cornwall for Brittany.

The verbs *be* and *have* are irregular.

Anguish is the King of Ireland.

Tristan has a beautiful old harp.

6 Complete the text with the Present Simple form of the verbs in brackets.

Brangwain a) ...is.. (be) Isolde's maid.

She b)............... (come) from Ireland.

She c)............... (have) long hair. She d)...............

(go) with Isolde to Cornwall when Isolde e)...............(marry) King Mark. Brangwain always f)............... (watch) the garden carefully when Tristan g)............... (visit) Isolde's room. When Isolde h)............... (kiss) Tristan in front of King Mark, the king i)...............(be) very angry. When Isolde j)...............(die) with Tristan in Brittany, Brangwain k) ....(bury) her next to her lover.

7 Write a text about Kurvenal with verbs in the Present Simple form. Use the text about Brangwain to help you.

Kurvenal .... servant. He .... Cornwall. He .... brown .... He .... Ireland after .... Morold. Kurvenal .... Tristan and Isolde 'The King is coming!' when King Mark .... hunting one night. When Tristan ...., Kurvenal .... Isolde.

GRAMMAR CHECK

Comparative adjectives

We add –er to most short adjectives.

tall – taller

When adjectives end in –e, we add –r.

nice – nicer

When adjectives end in consonant + –y, we change y to i and add –er.

hungry – hungrier

When adjectives end in a short vowel + consonant, we double the last consonant and add –er.

red – redder

With longer adjectives (other 2 syllable adjectives, or adjectives with 3 syllables or more) we put more before the adjective to make the comparative form.

interesting   *more interesting*

Some adjectives have an irregular comparative form.

good – better   *bad – worse*   *far – farther*

8 Write comparative sentences about Morold and Melot.

a Melot / bad / Morold *Melot is worse than Morold.*

b Morold / old / Melot ....

c Morold / angry / Melot ....

d Melot / fat / Morold ....

e Morold / unfriendly / Melot ....

f Morold / slow / Melot ....

g Melot / jealous / Morold ....

h Melot / careful / Morold ....

9 Write comparative sentences about Morold and Melot with these adjectives. Look at the sentences above to help you.

a good ....

b young ....

c quick ....

d friendly ....

GRAMMAR CHECK

Linkers: and, but, so, and because

and links two parts of a sentence with the same idea.

Isolde likes Ireland and she likes Cornwall, too.

but links two parts of a sentence with different ideas.

Isolde likes King Mark, but she loves Tristan.

so links two parts of a sentence talking about the result of something.

Peace between Ireland and Cornwall is important <u>so Isolde must marry King Mark</u>.

(result of first part of sentence)

because links two parts of a sentence talking about the reason for something.

Isolde feels bad in front of King Mark <u>because she and Tristan are in love</u>.

(reason for first part of sentence)

10 **Complete the sentences with *and*, *but*, *so*, or *because*.**

a Tristan fights Morold .....*and*..... he fights Melot later.

b Brangwain brings the potions to Isolde .... she doesn't want to kill her.

c Brangwain changes the poison for the love potion .... Tristan and Isolde don't die.

d Brangwain goes to King Mark's bed .... Isolde doesn't want to sleep with him.

e Everybody likes Tristan .... Melot hates him.

f Tristan dies sadly .... Blanche says, 'The sails are black.'

g Isolde can't live without Tristan .... she dies with him in Brittany.

h Kurvenal buries Tristan .... Brangwain buries Isolde.

DOMINOES THE STRUCTURED APPROACH TO READING IN ENGLISH

Dominoes is an enjoyable series of illustrated classic and modern stories in four carefully graded language stages – from Starter to Three – which take learners from beginner to intermediate level.

Each *Domino* reader includes:

- a **good story** to read and enjoy
- **integrated activities** to develop reading skills and increase active vocabulary
- **personalized projects** to make the language and story themes more meaningful
- **seven pages of grammar activities** for consolidation.

Each *Domino* pack contains a reader, plus a MultiROM with:

- a **complete audio recording of the story**, fully dramatized to bring it to life
- **interactive activities** to offer further practice in reading and language skills and to consolidate learning.

If you liked this Starter Level *Domino*, why not read these?

Rip Van Winkle & The Legend of Sleepy Hollow
Washington Irving

In the first of these stories, Rip Van Winkle sleeps for over twenty years, and then wakes up to a world that he no longer understands. In the other story, Ichabod Crane, the school teacher, meets a headless rider in the middle of a dark night. These two classic tales of the supernatural by Washington Irving have been popular for nearly two hundred years.

Book ISBN: 978 0 19 424702 3
MultiROM Pack ISBN: 978 0 19 424666 8

Changing Places
Alan Hines

Hal works at the zoo every day and his life isn't exciting – until he meets Tim.

Tim is a movie star. He has a difficult life, and he is unhappy – until he meets Hal.

But when they meet, and agree to change places, interesting things start to happen. And, by changing places, the two men learn what is truly important in their lives.

Book ISBN: 978 0 19 424708 5
MultiROM Pack ISBN: 978 0 19 424672 9

You can find details and a full list of books in the *Dominoes* catalogue and Oxford English Language Teaching Catalogue, and on the website: www.oup.com/elt

Teachers: see www.oup.com/elt for a full range of online support, or consult your local office.

	CEF	Cambridge Exams	IELTS	TOEFL iBT	TOEIC
Starter	A1	YLE Movers	–	–	–
Level 1	A1–A2	YLE Flyers/KET	3.0	–	–
Level 2	A2–B1	KET-PET	3.0-4.0	–	–
Level 3	B1	PET	4.0	57-06	550